Citizen Participation and Local Governance

Citizen Participation and Local Governance: Case Study of the Combined Harare Residents Association (Zimbabwe)

By

Jephias Mapuva

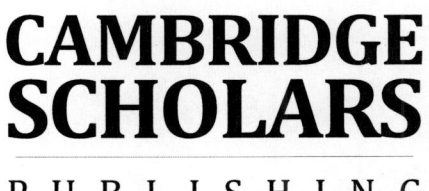

Citizen Participation and Local Governance:
Case Study of the Combined Harare Residents Association (Zimbabwe),
by Jephias Mapuva

This book first published 2010

Cambridge Scholars Publishing

12 Back Chapman Street, Newcastle upon Tyne, NE6 2XX, UK

British Library Cataloguing in Publication Data
A catalogue record for this book is available from the British Library

Copyright © 2010 by Jephias Mapuva

All rights for this book reserved. No part of this book may be reproduced, stored in a retrieval system, or transmitted, in any form or by any means, electronic, mechanical, photocopying, recording or otherwise, without the prior permission of the copyright owner.

ISBN (10): 1-4438-1954-9, ISBN (13): 978-1-4438-1954-1

TABLE OF CONTENTS

Chapter One 1
Introduction

Chapter Two 7
The Local Governance Discourse: A Global Perspective

Chapter Three 11
Democratic Discourses in Local Governance in Zimbabwe

Chapter Four 19
The Combined Harare Residents' Association (CHRA)

Chapter Five 39
CHRA and the Participatory Budgetary Process

Chapter Six 47
Interpretation and Implications of CHRA's Activities

Chapter Seven 51
Challenges Encountered and Lessons Learnt in Implementing Participatory Budgeting

Conclusion 53

References 55

CHAPTER ONE

INTRODUCTION

Preamble

Through devolution and decentralisation, central government has been able to hand down executive powers to local authorities; thereby bringing decision-making processes to the door step of the grassroots people. This has enabled citizens to participate in the administration of local authorities through contributions and presentations through the formation of residents associations. The Combined Harare Residents Association has made presentations to the local council and in the interim has been branded an opposition emissary. In budgetary processes, through residents associations, citizens have tried to influence budgetary allocations in favour of a pro-poor budget. However challenges have been encountered by residents associations as their membership suffers from a number of impediments ranging from low literacy and high poverty levels to the despotic nature of local authority officials. Additionally, some councillors have rudimentary understanding of local authority legislative provisions and modalities, let alone the low literacy levels of some of them. In recent years, CHRA has developed from a local association seeking to address issues of service delivery to one which attempts to influence issues of a national magnitude by compelling political authorities to address national issues such as economic development and constitutionalism.

***

The central argument of this book is based on the premise that citizens have the right to participate in governance processes within their geographical boundaries, as enshrined in ***Article 21*** of the Universal Declaration of Human and People's Rights and ***Article 13*** of the African Charter of Human and People's Rights, both of which concur that *"Every citizen shall have the right to participate freely in the government of his country, either directly or through freely chosen representatives in accordance with the provisions of the law"*. Consequently, it is on this premise that the author attempts to highlight and establish the extent to CHRA and the whole pro-democratic civil society movement alongside existing political, economic, social as well as environmental factors, have inculcated a culture of participation among its members.

Political developments in the decade 1980-1990 and the civic virtue in Zimbabwe

From the attainment of political independence in 1980, there were a number of political developments which militated against the ideals of the liberation struggle and the tenets of democracy in Zimbabwe. The liberation struggle had been executed in quest of universal suffrage, freedom and the adoption of democratic institutions and practices in the country. Armed with high hopes of a prosperous country where universal suffrage would be presented to all citizens as well as other civil liberties at the attainment of political independence in 1980, the developments of the post-colonial Zimbabwe were a disappointment to many citizens. The civil unrest in the early 1980s and the causalities incurred in the civil strife presented signs of what was to come and it cast doubts about the sustainability of the new democratic dispensation in the country. The signing of the Unity Accord in 1987 signalled the creation of a one-party state in Zimbabwe as the only formidable opposition-PF ZAPU was absorbed by ZANU PF in the process. Numerous constitutional amendments to suit ZANU PF were effected with constitutional Amendment 17 providing an Executive President with enormous arbitrary powers. Although all these developments caused dis-comfort within the general citizenry and civil society movement of the day, it is not surprising that many civic groups went as far as issues out carefully structured statements of discontent, especially given the polarization of society on the aftermath of the Matabeleland civil unrest where over 20 000 people had died, and many were either maimed and/or displaced. Only church-related civic groups such as the Catholic Commission for Justice and Peace (CCJP), conscious of their religious obligations, dared to undertake an investigation of the Matabeleland Massacres and established the atrocious manner in which the unrest was handled and falling short of calling it an ethnic cleansing exercise by the military. This saw more civic groups joining the CCJP in condemning government's military operation in Matabeleland, with ZimRights joining later to deploy human rights activists to ascertain human rights violation in the military escapade in Matabeleland. Other political developments which further infringed on people's rights included the Land Reform Programme, which was executed on the backdrop of political violence and disorderliness with due disregard of individual property rights. Although on the surface these developments might not relevant to CHRA, what the author seeks to achieve is to express the view that these political developments did not measure up to the tenets of democracy, but that they were laying a foundation and justification for the creation of a multi-faceted civil society movement capable of addressing all areas of democracy such as suffrage, human rights, good governance and the rule of law. Even at local government level, residents began to view the political establishment of the 1980s and 1990 as not only inconsiderate, but one which had shifted from the ideals of the liberation struggle which were to establish a participatory democracy and people-driven country characterised by equitable allocation of resources.

Although it was at a time when opposition to government was detrimental and suicidal, many social movements, civic groups and NGOs were formed and existing ones beginning to re-align their objectives which had initially been non-confrontational and began to call upon government to account and respect human rights. It was in the midst of these calls that human rights began to take centre stage with relevant groups like the Zimbabwe Human Rights Organisation (**ZimRights**) was formed in 1992. The civil society even began to diversify towards the end of the 20th century and the dawn of the 21th saw the formation of feminist organizations like Women Of Zimbabwe Arise (**WOZA**) presenting a threat to government through composite demands for government to address any anomalies in the political and economic spheres ranging from the availability of basic food commodities, making education affordable for the poor to restoring democracy in the country. The 'expropriation' of white commercial farms signalled the government and ZANU PF's preparedness to contravene property rights of individuals. The holding of the National Referendum in 1999, the first-ever referendum to be held in post-colonial Zimbabwe heralded the beginning of a new era as government had shown the first ever signs of succumbing to pressure from civil society for a new constitution to replace the Lancaster House Constitution of 1979. It was also the first sign that the ZAN PF government was losing grip and becoming increasingly unpopular with the electorate. The period also heralded the increasing popularity of civics at different spheres of government. At local government level, residents' associations began to join in the bandwagon of groups demanding improved service delivery, respect for human rights and the need to address the political and economic crises that were bedevilling the country for the last decade, with the Combined Harare Residents Association

(**CHRA**) having been the most prominent. In large cities, residents associations began to consolidate through forming coalitions. In smaller towns once defunct residents associations began to re-emerge while news were formed in towns that had not had any representations at local government level. Others like CHRA and BURA began to re-align their objectives to go beyond local governance and transcending their boundaries to clamour for the resolution of the constitutional crisis, and the improvement of the national economy, as well as the need for the political parties to accept election results in both local government and national elections. It is therefore the purpose of this book to establish the extent to which civil society institutions like residents associations have enhanced citizen participation in governance processes and how local governance have transformed during the tumultuous years of the 1990s which were characterised by political and economic crises and diminishing participatory spaces.

Residents' Associations as a Conduit for Citizen Participation

Residents associations are an old concept, having started during the colonial era when due to the increase in the number of Africans in urban areas, an interest arouse around their conditions of living. These associations have been associated with urban dwellings and during colonial days, with poor living conditions such as over crowdedness, establishment and living conditions in squatter camps (informal settlements) as well as shortage of safe drinking waters and other proper sanitary conditions befitting human habitation. Local authorities became increasingly under pressure from residents to address these issues.

Consequently, urban development and human settlement has brought to the fore issues of good living conditions, proper service delivery and good governance. Historically, associational life amongst Africans in the towns tended to be as temporal and ephemeral as the periods spent by migrant workers in the early urban settlements (Moyo, Makumbe and Raftopoulos, 2000:23) and were spaces "...coterminous with modernization and therefore antithetical to African tradition and control (Yoshikuni, 1999, in Moyo & Makumbe, 2000:23). The high rates of urban population growth raised the need for a corresponding increase in the provision of quality services. However, urban local authorities lack adequate resources to meet the demand for quality services, which is on the rise as a consequence of political emancipation, high literacy rates and increased global communication. The challenge facing decision-makers has been to develop models of local governance that can best facilitate the involvement of civil society and how much civil society can contribute to the establishment of good governance in a sustainable way. For Mamadou (1996:79), the challenges of local governance emanates from "...the institutional disconnect between formal modern institutions transplanted from outside and indigenous, informal institutions rooted in local culture namely entire government machinery, from ministries to local governments". It is this 'disconnect' which the Combined Harare Residents' Association has attempted to address by calling on the local authority to account. Matovu, (2006:69) notes that increasing demands for local government transformation and decentralization "...have opened up spaces for better participation in decision-making processes and administration". In this vein, the Combined Harare Residents Association's activities in attempting to enhance citizen participation in budgetary processes as well as other democratic overtures will be deliberated upon.

Chapter Two

The Local Governance Discourse: A Global Perspective

Local governance has, in recent years, rose in prominence as industrialisation and urbanisation have equally increased in intensity, resulting in an influx of rural-urban migration, mostly in search of better employment opportunities and other 'greener pastures'. This influx into urban areas has equally put pressure on existing infrastructure most of which has been in existence since the colonial times. The pressure so exerted on existing infrastructure has resulted in sewer bursts and shortage of housing for the increasing urban population as well as shortage of safe drinking water. Energy consumption has also increased resulting in power outrages and regular power cuts. Given global recession and diminishing resources, governments and local authorities have been unable to provide for their urban population, resulting in appalling services deliveries to citizens. In an attempt to be part of the solution, citizens have demanded that they be made part of the problem-solving mechanism in affairs that affect their livelihoods and demanding a place in the decision-making process within their constituencies.

Unlike in Africa where urban development initiatives and legislation are country-specific, in Europe local governance is guided by regional legislative instruments which all countries concerned should abide by. The European Union has a charter, the European Charter, which guides member countries on how local governance should be conducted within their specific constituencies with emphasis being on good local governance and the inculcation of a culture of democratic local governance. In an effort to articulate local governance, the Charter employs *decentralisation* "involving the delegation of a range of powers, competencies and resources from the central government to elected local (sub-national) governments" (Charter, 2007:2); *de-concentration* which is the delegation of administrative functions from the State to local non-elected public structures (Charter, 2007:2), as well as *local democratic governance* which espouses and encourages an equal participation of all stakeholders of a territory (State, citizen civil society, private sector), reinforces accountability towards citizens and responsiveness to social demands in seeking to satisfy the general interest.

Civil Society, Decentralisation and Local Governance in the African context

The local government transformation and decentralization processes underway in Sub-Saharan Africa have opened space to better participate in decision-making processes and administration (Matovu, 2006:5). The challenge facing decision-makers has been to develop models of local governance that can best facilitate the involvement of civil society as well as how and how much civil society can contribute to the establishment of good governance in a sustainable way. Scholars have provided varied definitions of the concept of civil society, with the most common definition referring to civil society as organizations through which citizens participate and exert influence over public life. Manor (1999:34) maintains that it can be understood as "organized interests with a significant degree of autonomy from the state". Swilling (1992:4) offers the view that civil society consists of locally constituted voluntary organizations, which have the capacity to influence and even determine the structure of power and the allocation of resources. These are institutions that exert pressure and control as "watch-dogs" on state institutions in the area of governance and development, and jealously guard their autonomy and identity. Mamadou (1996:78) argues that many African countries are characterized by an institutional disconnect between formal modern institutions transplanted from outside and indigenous, informal institutions rooted in local culture. Formal institutions include the entire government machinery, from ministries to local governments. Civil society organizations exist as political organizations, trade unions, human rights groups, community-based organizations, and others. As a rule, civil society organizations adhere to the following principles: participation, transparency, accountability, equity, effectiveness and efficiency, strategic vision, and good management.

In theory, a vibrant civil society can contribute to effective institutional development and democratic decentralization, enhance the responsiveness of government institutions, increase the information flow between government and the people, make development projects more sustainable, enhance accountability, transparency and integrity—all of which constitute good governance. However, considering the challenges that face local governance, it might be difficult for government to fully embrace civil society as a pillar of democratic decentralization.

The socio-political and economic crises that engulfed Sub-Saharan Africa in the 1990s has persuaded state and non-state actors to collective review policy and institutional mechanisms for delivering services and foster development. Citizens demand quality services, while city managers lack the resources and morale to perform. One of the reasons civil society groups sprung up in the 1990s was the incapability of local governments to deliver services and fight against poverty and environmental destruction on their own.

It is unfortunate, as country experiences reveal, that the two parties (state and civil society) have difficulties engaging in a productive relationship. Heyden (1983:13) had earlier observed that in most African countries, governmental staff tended to be quite arbitrary in their approach to the people for whom they were designing or executing policies. If the people questioned or resisted arbitrary tactics, the officials resorted to intimidation or other measures aimed at punishing the vocal citizens. This culture continues unabated in spite of decentralization and democratization of governance. In Uganda public officials are wary of civic associations, not least because of their role as vocal advocates for the disadvantaged, and are therefore reluctant to allow them to play a more active role in public affairs. Councillors tend to believe that civil society thrives on sowing seeds of political discontent and on challenging the legitimacy of the councils. In Zimbabwe, the liberation background of the country which forced it to adopt a socialist/communist stance, tend to view non-state actors as saboteurs who should be guarded against or even avoided at all costs. Consequently local governance in Zimbabwe is heavily politicised with the ruling political party calling the shots to municipal authorities.

CHAPTER THREE

DEMOCRATIC DISCOURSES IN LOCAL GOVERNANCE IN ZIMBABWE

Generally, democratic discourses in governance are informed by such practices as *participation, decentralisation* and *devolution* of authority from central government to local structures and to institutions such as municipalities herein referred to as local authorities. Accordingly, terms such as governance; participation and participatory democracy; local governance; decentralisation and devolution have come to dominate the [local] governance parlance and discourse. Governance is about how governments and other social organizations interact, how they relate to citizens, and how decisions are taken in a complex world (Graham, & Plumptre, 2003:2), and involves "...the manner in which power is exercised in the management of a country's economic and social development" (World Bank, 1994; UNDP, 1997). Hyden and Court (1992:19) view governance as *"...the formation and stewardship of the formal and informal rules that regulate the public realm, the arena in which state as well as economic and social actors interact to make decisions"*. Folscher, in World Bank (2007:243) notes that increased state effectiveness in service delivery and the creation of citizen participatory spaces is evident of good governance.

In participatory democracy "...citizens should have direct roles in public choices or at least engage more deeply with substantive political issues and be assured that officials will be responsive to their concerns and judgments" (Cohen and Fung 2004:27). Gaventa (2006:150) regards participatory governance as "...deepening democratic engagement through the participation of citizens in the processes of [local] governance". In participatory democracy citizens should be actively involved in matters that affect them by demanding accountability from the state ensuring government's responsiveness to service delivery and other societal needs (Jones and Weale, 1999:91). This justifies why citizens call on elected officials to account.

The World Bank (2007:191) points out that "...specific legislation governs sub-national governments through the constitution which recognizes local government and prescribes the need for civic participation in local matters". Zimbabwe's local government system dates back to 1891 when the Salisbury Sanitary Board was established under the Urban Councils Act to look at the sanitary needs of an increasing African population in the then capital city of Salisbury (Wekwete, 1988.1:19). The Urban Councils Act was preceded by the Municipal Act (1930). A number of other pieces of legislation facilitated the carrying out of most of additional functions by Urban Councils. For example, the Services Levy Act (Chapter 78) empowered Urban Councils to impose a form of levy on employers of African labour, which funds could be used to subsidize housing and urban transport services for Africans in urban areas (Palley, 1996:630). Increased disenchantment with ZANU PF rule led to a vote of no confidence in most ZANU PF councilors across the country, leading to partisan amendments to the Urban Councils Act to further empower the Minister of Local Government, a ZANU PF apologist to disadvantage citizens in numerous ways, including dismissing democratically elected mayors and councilors in most cities and arbitrarily appointing Commissions to run the affairs of urban areas, a move which was disapproved by CHRA on many occasions. However, the dynamic nature of Zimbabwe's political landscape brought about principally by the democratic decay that has characterized Zimbabwe's politics towards the end of the 1990s has brought all the above cited benefits to African urbanites to an end as the state became increasingly entrenched in a *laager mentality*.

In Zimbabwe, all urban areas are divided into high-density (former African) and low-density (former European) areas. As the terms imply, most middle and low income earners reside in high-density areas, and the areas are mostly characterised by large family units and high poverty and literacy levels, hence much more demand for service delivery and activism is found in these residential areas. These are areas which have often formed the bedrock of resistance and a source of dissenting voices from an increasingly restive population as the residents are most affected by poor service delivery. This argument is supported by Makumbe (1998:67) who argues that "urban areas tend to have a significantly higher level of political consciousness than rural areas, at least in Zimbabwe". Makumbe further notes that resident' associations "have become fora for opposing national government policies, especially those that impinge on citizens' rights" (Makumbe, 1998:87).

The impact of the Structural Adjustment Programme has left many casualties in its wake because much of the retrenchments and school drop outs occurred during this time, thereby exacerbating poverty levels among the urban citizens, mostly in high density areas and informal settlements as the state became increasingly bankrupt an could not afford to subsidise basic commodities and services. This happened on the backdrop of an unprecedented increase in quality and improved service delivery by citizens I urban areas, giving residents associations homework as to how they were going to engage local authorities on the same issue. High poverty levels in urban areas and a demand for better service delivery against the backdrop of worsening service provision in all urban areas brought about by the sanctions imposed on the country by western governments further exacerbated the quagmire in which local authorities found themselves in. Subsequently, this catch22 situation contributed to the creation and emergence of a militant urban population whose knowledge of citizen entitlements went beyond that of the early 1980s when citizens treated the then ruling party, ZANU PF and government as entities beyond reproach. These appalling living conditions and low living standards constructed an urban population whose resolve to meet their objectives of demanding good service delivery from the local authorities helped them employ mobilisation strategies akin to those utilised during the colonial era for equitable fair living and working conditions. All these factors held implications for democratic representation of the citizens residing in the different urban residential areas.

Urbanization and the rise of civil society

As Africa's urban settlements grew in both number and size faster than in any other region of the world, recent reviews of urbanization trends have shown that the urban population of Africa is growing by 6 percent per annum, twice as fast as that of Latin America or East Asia (Bossuyt, 2000:6). It is projected that at the current rate, the urban population is likely to reach 500 million by the year 2025 due to increased massive migration from rural to urban centres, in addition to natural growth within the urban centres themselves. The high rates of urban population growth raise the need for a corresponding increase in the provision of services. However, urban local authorities have always been characterised by lack of adequate resources to meet the demand for quality services, which is on the rise as a consequence of political emancipation, high literacy rates and increased global communication.

Lwanga-Ntale, Golooba-Mutebi and Taaka, (1999:46) have cited various factors as the cause of civil society's rapid growth in urban areas. Firstly, urban citizens are more enlightened and sophisticated than their rural counterparts. As a result, they are interested in establishing independent space outside the direct control of the state to escape political and economic oppression and improve their living conditions. Secondly, indigenous associations receive external assistance from international organizations which enhance their propensity to engage the state and improve their operations. Thirdly, the conditionalities imposed on governments to liberalize and democratize lead to state withdrawal from the provision of basic services, thereby giving citizens the opportunity to exercise some control over their lives.

Associational life in urban areas in colonial Zimbabwe: a historical overview

Industrialisation and the desire for colonial authorities to derive maximum profit from their industrial concerns led to the need for cheap labour. Ordinarily the existence of Africans in urban areas was prohibited under colonial legislation unless they were providing cheap labour in mines and factories. Colonial authorities saw it necessary to have some control of Africans in urban areas by putting in place laws that would govern their freedoms of association, movement, and even assembly. This justifies the enactment of laws which required every African to possess a pass indicating their names and that of their employer where applicable. With the advent of increased industrialization in the 1930s and 1940s, the number of Africans in urban areas correspondingly increased, leading to the development of formal settlements. Associational life amongst Africans in the towns tended to be as temporal and ephemeral as the periods spent by migrant workers in the early urban settlements (Moyo, Makumbe and Raftopoulos, 2000:23). For the colonial state, up until the 1940s, "...the urban space was considered European space in which blacks were to be allowed for short periods of time" (Moyo, 2001:32). In the language of the colonialists, the urban spaces were coterminous with modernization and therefore antithetical to African tradition and control (Yoshikuni, 1999, in Moyo & Makumbe, 2000:23). It is therefore not surprising that Africans were largely located in rural areas where reserves had been created for them by the Land Apportionment Act of 1930, and those in urban areas were settled in designated areas with limited recreational and housing facilities.

With further increased industrialization, the number of workers in urban areas also increased and this led to the development of larger cities like Salisbury and Bulawayo that had large industrial concerns. This also led to the formation and prominence of organizations residents' associations that would engage authorities in improving the living conditions of urban residents. However, in the early days, the residents associations were limited in scope and attempted to address those issues that the colonial administration did not considerer sensitive, such as demanding equality with whites in terms of job opportunities and living standards. The emergence of residents associations in tandem with trade unionism gave birth to militancy as the colonial administration refused to consider Africans as equal human beings. The militant spirit manifested itself through more demands for citizens' rights in all aspects of life. This was the genesis of trade unionism which according to the Industrial Conciliation Act of 1951 was illegal. With the advent of greater industrialization and urbanization in the 1940s and 1950s more African migrated to urban areas in search of job opportunities, resulting in an upsurge in the African population in towns. As industrialisation further grew in leaps and bounds, more labour was required and recruited, leading to the growth of cities. This had a knock-on effect on the formation of new groups like township resident associations which emerged initially with the aim of fighting for the rights of urban residents, but later working in league with the emerging liberation movements for political emancipation of the African people not only in urban areas, but even in rural areas. With the passage of time, these resident associations began to diversify their engagement with the colonial administration by challenging the white economic and political order. They began to demand for the observance of human rights, universal suffrage and enfranchisement, political representation and improved living and working conditions for Africans.

With the attainment of political independence in Zimbabwe in 1980, much of the colonial legislation was reversed in an attempt to democratise local governance. Through the Urban Councils Act (1993) residents were empowered to form residents associations through which citizens would make representations to the local authority. These are associations through which residents can participate and influence the decision-making processes in the local governance by having a say in the affairs that affect their lives, especially given that "the post-independence local government system in Zimbabwe was deliberately designed to create a one-party state with the ruling ZANU PF as the one party (Makumbe, 1998:97). However the legacy brought about by the liberation created a scenario where everything and every functionary had to be ZANU PF. Up until the late 1990s, most urban councils were staffed with ZANU PF supporters and even senior positions such as those of the Town Clerk, Chamber Secretary or mayor (though ceremonial position) were packed with ruling party supporters, functionaries and operatives. Wekwete, (1988) in Makumbe,(1998:86) concurred with the affinity between ZANU (PF) and the whole local government structure by asserting that "the whole local government structure in Zimbabwe is a carbon copy of the ZANU (PF) structure". Councillors and other municipal council officials were elected or appointed on a partisan basis - on the basis of the strength of support for the then ZANU (PF) party. This was necessitated by ZANU PF's willingness to exclude any voices of dissent from the operations of municipal and city councils. Municipal bylaws and other processes such as municipal budgetary processes were handed over to residents. In some cases, although the Urban Councils Acts requires that the local authority places and advertisement in the media publicising any municipal decisions and budgets for the following year, they have always been aware of the fact that up until the early 1990s, residents in urban areas did not bother themselves about having to partake in the budgetary processes of council.

Attempts at forming residents associations during the early 1980s were viewed by the ruling party as unnecessary. However, continued poor service delivery, water reticulation and sewer bursts uncollected refuse strengthened residents' resolve to solve their own problems with cities and town councils. This resulted in residents having to revisit the concept of residents associations which had existed during the colonial era and to enhance and overhaul the associations into vibrant formations that would not only confine themselves to immediate needs of towns and cities, but extended their demands to incorporate issues of both local and central governance. This is the premise on which Residents Associations in large cities like Harare, Bulawayo, Mutare and Gweru were formed and modelled. Residents such as the Combined Harare Association have contributed to the restoration, promotion and sustenance of elements of democratic institutions through enhancing citizen participation in governance processes. Recent political developments in which the opposition Movement for Democratic Change (MDC) dominated most of urban (and even rural councils) have precipitated a paradigm shift in the composition of most urban councils. This case study would help the author to articulate the extent to which the formation has enhanced citizen participation through engaging government on the plight of urban residents brought about poor service delivery. The book will also explore how the formation has mobilized the residents around its broad objective of engaging government and campaigning not only for improved service delivery in local government, but to restore democracy in the country through exhorting their members to participate in the constitution outreach programmes, partake in all electoral processes and be involved in the constitution-making process. This mandate by CHRA has out span its initial functions and operations which, mostly hinged on local governance and service delivery.

In Zimbabwe, all urban areas are divided into high-density (former African) and low-density (former European) areas. As the terms imply, most middle and low income earners reside in high-density areas, and the areas are mostly characterised by large family units and high levels of poverty, hence much more incidences of service breakdown, poor service delivery protests and a source of voices of dissent. The impact of the Structural Adjustment Programme left many casualties in that much of the retrenchments and school drop outs occurred during this time, thereby exacerbating poverty levels among the urban citizens. This has created an increased demand on urban authorities for improved service delivery. High poverty levels in urban areas and a demand for better service delivery against the backdrop of worsening service provision in all urban areas brought about by the sanctions has culminated in the emergence of a militant urban population whose knowledge of their rights as citizens goes beyond that of the early 1980s when citizens treated the ruling party and government as entities beyond reproach, a population whose resolve to meet their objectives could see them employing any mobilisation strategy available to them. All these factors have implications for democratic representation of the citizens residing in the two different urban residential areas. The fact that the two groups of people reside in urban settings have a bearing on their political consciousness, as noted by Makumbe (1998:67) who argues that "urban areas tend to have a significantly higher level of political consciousness than rural areas, at least in Zimbabwe". The political developments in Zimbabwe, coupled by high levels of poverty and a hyperinflationary environment have overshadowed these differences as the two groups of people experience the same political power service delivery and poverty levels brought about by sanctions on the country. It is against this background that the author explores CHRA as a manifestation of a representative residents association whose mandate has not been confined to local governance but with the setting in of democratic decay and diminishing participatory spaces, in Zimbabwe, at least from the late 1990s. CHRA also represents a microcosm of sections of the civil society movement in the country that due to the gravity of democratic decay in the country had to re-align their objectives and operations in tandem with the requirements of participatory democracy where citizens are required to involve in all governance processes in the country. However, the cause behind the formation of residents associations and much of the civil society movement have been frustrated and worsened by the ZANU PF government's pessimistic view that residents' associations "have become fora for opposing national government policies" (Makumbe, 1998:87). This has left social movements, civil society organisations in limbo as persecutions and surveillance became the order of the day. Although these have been setbacks, but citizens have continued to make these associations and other civic groups operational on the backdrop of forms of harassment and persecutions by state security agents.

Chapter Four

The Combined Harare Residents' Association (CHRA)

The World Bank (2007:191) points out that "...specific legislation governs sub-national governments through the constitution which recognizes local government and prescribes the need for civic participation in local matters". Zimbabwe's Local Government system dates back to 1891 when the Salisbury sanitary Board was established (Wekwete, 1988.1:19). The Urban Councils Act was preceded by the Municipal Act (1930). A number of other pieces of legislation facilitated the carrying out of most of additional functions by Urban Councils. For example, the Services Levy Act (Chapter 78) have enabled Urban Councils to impose a levy on employers of African labour, which funds can be used to subsidize housing and urban transport services for Africans in urban areas (Palley, 1996:630). However, the dynamic nature of Zimbabwe's political landscape brought about principally by the democratic decay that has characterized Zimbabwe's politics in recent years has brought all the above cited benefits to African urbanites to an end.

Post-independence amendments to the colonial Urban Councils Act (1973), Chapter 214 resulted in the democratization of the Local Government system by removing racial discrimination pertaining to representation and tenure in urban areas (Wekwete, 1988:20), through the incorporation of former local government areas or African Townships into Urban Council areas (Jordan, 1984:9). This resulted in the enactment of the Urban Councils Act in 1980 and subsequently amended in 1983, 1986, 1993 and 1996. The Act empowers citizens to form residents' associations, through which citizens would influence policy making and other local governance processes. This has seen the creation of the numerous residents' associations, all of which are affiliates of the Combined Harare Residents' Association. The Combined Harare Residents Associations is the umbrella body of the capital's residents associations and in recent years has encompassed and affiliated residents associations from different towns and cities in Zimbabwe. For purposes of readers, the CHRA will be representative of all residents associations in the country and will act as a microcosm of social movements in Zimbabwe.

CHRA has been taken as a case study because of its magnitude, representing so many satellite residents associations and households around the country. Secondly, the CHRA represents people of all walks of life ranging from the rich to the poor, the formally employed to those in informal sector, the old and the young, the grassroots citizens to the professionals, pensioners and even lodgers, the business sector and the formal households, the Central Business Districts of various towns and cities as well as different suburbs (low-density, medium density and high-density). CHRA also represents those in informal settlements like Epworth where residents' propensity is curtailed by low levels of education. On education and participation the level of education, Shah (2007:253) notes that "educational attainment is less important as a determinant of participation than citizens' grasp of their rights to engage in individual and collective action and to hold state actors to account". This leaves citizens with an inborn intuition to want to be part of a solution to problems bedevilling them.

Preamble to the formation of the Combined Harare Residents Association (CHRA)

In Zimbabwe, with increased industrialization, the number of workers in urban areas grew, leading to the development of larger cities like Salisbury and Bulawayo that had large industrial concerns. This also led to the formation and prominence of organizations residents' associations that would engage authorities in improving the living conditions of urban residents. With the passage of time, these resident associations began to challenge the white economic and political order.

Residents associations are attempts by residents to participate in the local governance of their affairs. Zimbabwe's Local Government system dates back to 1891 when the Salisbury Sanitary Board was established (Wekwete, 1988.1:19). The Urban Councils Act was preceded by the Municipal Act (1930). A number of other pieces of legislation facilitated the carrying out of most of additional functions by Urban Councils. For example, the Services Levy Act (Chapter 78) have enabled Urban Councils to impose a levy on employers of African labour, which funds can be used to subsidize housing and urban transport services for Africans in urban areas (Palley, 1996:630). However, the dynamic nature of Zimbabwe's political landscape brought about principally by the democratic decay that has characterized Zimbabwe's politics in recent years has brought all the above cited benefits to African urbanites to an end.

Residents' Associations are voluntary organizations that thrive on the commitment of the citizens to participate. Participation in these voluntary associations has attracted a lot of controversy in recent years with some associations being accused of extensions of opposition political parties. Irvin and Stansbury (2005:59) argue that "...because citizen participants are not paid for their time,[such] committees may be dominated by strongly partisan participants whose livelihood or values are strongly affected by the decisions being made, or by those who live comfortably enough to allow them to participate regularly". It has been argued that "...citizen-participation committees such as resident associations, are usually overpopulated with members of the top socio-economic group" (Weber 2000:59) because "...the main priorities [of those from the low-income groups] are to provide for their families, not spend time in meetings" (Russell and Vidler, 2000, in Irvin and Stansbury, 2005:59). However, the composition of CHRA goes against this assumption as the organization is populated by the grieved poverty-stricken citizen in urban areas whose interest is not confined to improved service delivery, but the restoration of democratic institutions in the country, hence their involvement in national programmes like the constitution-making process, election monitoring and petitioning the Minister of Local Government against dismissal of democratically-elected councillors in any town and city in the country.

The author has cited the CHRA into the discussion of local governance and as a microcosm of residents associations throughout the country because of its magnitude which is a coalition of numerous similar-minded local government endeavours to enhance citizen participatory tools. Firstly the organization takes cognizance of many households in the country. Secondly, the CHRA represents people of all walks of life ranging from the rich to the poor, the formally employed to those in informal sector, the old and the young, the grassroots to the professionals, pensioners and even lodgers, the business sector and the formal households, the Central Business Districts of various towns surrounding the capital city as well as different suburbs (low-density, medium density and high-density) as has been cited before.

However, while there has been evidence to support the effectiveness of residents associations insofar as influencing policy is concerned,

developments theorists argue to the contrary. The World Bank (2000:56) argues that the ordinary citizens do not have the capacity and ability to influence public policy. To facilitate citizen participation, an appropriate and enabling environment should be created where human rights are observed, democratic structures put in place, the constitution is upheld, and the need to allow civil society unlimited access to the citizenry. It points out that "…the poor are often untouched by formal civil society organizations; instead they rely on a host of informal associations within their communities that often lack the capacity to influence government decision making, and which are by-and-large limited in number, resources and leverage". However, this is rather a discouraging remark by developmental multilateral institutions that should be canvassing for participatory democracy through citizen involvement in national and local programmes and decision-making processes.
Post-independence amendments to the colonial Urban Councils Act (1996, Chapter 214 resulted in the democratization of the local government system by removing racial discrimination pertaining to representation and tenure in urban areas (Wekwete, 1988:20), through the incorporation of former local government areas or African Townships into Urban Council areas (Jordan, 1984:9) leading to the enactment of the Urban Councils Act in 1980.

In 1999, six neighbourhood residents' groups-some dating back to the 1940s- merged to form CHRA. The Combined Harare Residents Associations as the umbrella body of the capital's residents associations and in recent years has encompassed and affiliated residents associations from different towns and cities in Zimbabwe.

CHRA is guided by its vision which is:

"To be an effective watchdog and vehicle for good governance in Harare and a model for advocacy.

Its mission statement is:

"To represent and support all residents of Harare by advocating for effective, transparent and affordable municipal and other services and quality facilities on a professional, non partisan basis".

In 2005, the association re-aligned its objectives from those of merely being a rate payers association to that of being"...an expression of the growing power of residents' collective action and ...an effective monitor of the activities of elected councilors as well as municipal (Davies, 2005:7). In 1999, a trust was formed and CHRA was registered as a civil society organization. In 2000, an advocacy centre was established as a way facilitating and engaging local authority as well as central government on issues that affect residents within CHRA area of jurisdiction and beyond. The constitution of CHRA portrays the organization as one whose objective is *"to promote and protect the rights of residents of Harare* (CHRA, 2006a). CHRA's preoccupation with urban governance, as cited by Kamete (2009:62), is amplified by its maxim which reads "CHRA for Enhanced Civic Participation in Local Governance". According to (Kamete, 2009:62) CHRA has set local governance-related objectives as;

- *advocating for effective, transparent and affordable municipal and other services and quality facilities;*
- *making representations to and liaising with Harare City Council, city councilors, Central Government or any ministries, government departments or other public institutions concerning matters affecting residents of Harare and is environs;*
- *promoting and encouraging public awareness and participation by residents in local governance issues; and*
- *doing all things necessary to protect and promote the rights and interests of residents.*

Summed up, it is these objectives that define CHRA's "core focus", which is "...to develop participatory approaches to local governance and demand for accountability" (Davies, 2005:10).

In 2000, an Advocacy Centre was established as CHRA's secretariat which oversees the day-to-day running of the affairs of the movement. In addition to the secretariat, CHRA has structures which enables it to consult with residents as well as the general citizenry on pertinent issues like those pertaining to good governance, not only at local government levels, but nationally. These are the General Council, Standing Committees.

The General Council (GC) is the supreme decision making body of the Association in between the Annual General Meeting (AGM). The GC meets every month and is constituted by the Ward Chairpersons and

Coordinators from the Association's ward committees and the Management Committee.

The Association has the following six (6) Standing Committees (S.C):

1. Programmes
2. Finance
3. Information and Publicity
4. Legal
5. Membership
6. Environment

Each one of these Standing Committees deals with matters that falls within is armpits as the names suggest.

The S.C makes recommendations on programming and activities to the Secretariat. Ward Chairpersons and Coordinators volunteer into Standing Committees. The Chairperson of each S.C sits in the Management Committee.

In addition to these structures, CHRA has representations in different wards, from where it is able to reach out to residents and be in a position to access their needs and allow them to participate in the running of the City of Harare. In an effort to reach out to citizens and educate them on issues of participatory governance and their rights, CHRA has come up with projects. The projects are, Grassroots Advocacy Project, Capacity Building Project as well as the Information Blitz Project[1].

4.1 The Grassroots Advocacy Initiative Project

The Grassroots Advocacy Initiative Project enables CHRA to disseminate and gather information pertaining to the welfare of ratepayers and their subsequent participation in local governance in Mbare[2] and beyond. The Grassroots Advocacy Initiative seeks to coordinate advocacy initiatives, gather and disseminate information. CHRA acts as a public response

---

[1] CHRA 2009
[2] Mbare is a high density suburb in Harare and is home to both low-income and middle income groups.

mechanism to the various forms crises that might occur in the capital and in demanding for quality municipal service and elections.

Key activities include Ward Committee meetings where the project facilitates committee meetings for the Association ward structures in Mbare (Ward 3, 4, 11, and 12) for the purposes of developing and coordinating implementation of their activities. The Association also facilitates Core Group discussion meetings at which the Association convenes core group meetings to monitor the implementation of resolutions and action plans by the ward committee. The Associations also undertakes campaigns where it coordinates popular action and clean up campaigns in Mbare in line with committee resolutions. Information packaging and distribution forms a vital component campaign and conscientisation tool where the Association is engaged in the production of *'The Mbare Resident'* a bi-weekly newsletter that highlights the state of service delivery in Mbare, CHRA initiatives and local residents action plans and *'The Mbare Weekly'* which focuses on current developments in local governance and other municipal issues.

4.2 Capacity Building Project

The Capacity Building Project focuses on raising the level of civic awareness, participation in the formulation, implementation and monitoring of policies. Additionally, the Association is involved in research and deepening knowledge and information systems in participatory democracy. It is also involved with lobbying and advocacy for democratic local government pro-people centred policies. Most importantly, for mobilisation purposes, CHRA is involved in developing a critical mass that will be the vanguard for democracy and transparent governance as well as fostering transparency and accountability in local government (CHRA, 2006).

Key activities include the involve CHRA's capacity building initiatives which incorporate local governance research and policy analysis. Current research activities focus on reviewing the political framework in the country that defines civic participation, analysis of local governance legislation and best practices in local governance locally, regionally and even internationally. This capacity building initiative also focuses on defining the framework for enhanced civic participation in local governance, establishing a research pool and extensive library on local governance and defining an alternative local government legislative framework (and policy) in a democratic dispensation. This is on the backdrop of current restrictive legislation which among other things includes the prohibition of protest action, curtailed freedoms such as those of assembly, expression and even gatherings without police approval. According to CHRA, such restrictive pieces of legislation have had a debilitating impact on their consultative meetings with residents.

Under its Training and Capacity Building, the Association runs the Training for Transformation (T4T) sessions to its wider membership in partnership with stakeholders. The T4T targets the Association's leadership at all levels (Ward, General Council and Management Committee). The training focuses on developing leadership skills on community leaders to enhance their competences in the development and governance matters. Training is also done around best practice and alternative frameworks. There is also a component of staff and organizational development to facilitate the formulation of shared vision. The Association has secured mobile offices for the purpose of facilitating convenience in the administration of ward activities and programmes across the 45 municipal wards within the CHRA jurisdiction. The mobile offices include; trunks, receipt books and stationery (CHRA, 2006).

In addition to the above mentioned endeavours, the Association has enhanced their outreach programmes through the use of the media as a way to reach out to its constituency. They have facilitated communication with their constituency through running media campaigns on topical local governance issues and through the development of audio, visual and print aids as part of the broader media strategy. The project also facilitates public meetings on consultative and key positions of the Association. Added to this, CHRA runs municipal budget works to its wider membership in order to equip and enhance residents understating on municipal budgeting and participation in budget formulation processes.

Lobbying and advocacy have formed part of CHRA's core business with stakeholders and central government. The Association runs lobbying and advocacy work targeted at the Zimbabwean Parliament, Parliamentarians and the Parliamentary Portfolio Committee on Local Government through submissions and discussions on local government budget votes, legislative and policy reform issues. The key objectives of the Parliamentary Advocacy are aimed at entrenching public consultation and participation culture in all strata of governance. The Association also spearheads the development of scorecards for monitoring elected representatives' performance. This monitoring mechanism for councillors have made them more effective and hardworking because periodically, the councillors are called upon by CHRA and residents to account for issues like deteriorating service delivery trends that seem to have become the norm in recent years. Monthly workshops with media personnel and the production of visual and audio material are part of the communication activities. This is intended to bring the nation and sister residents associations in other towns and cities up to speed with developments in Harare, and to share information on local governance with other residents associations.

4.3 Information Blitz Project

The Information Blitz Project s also been instituted by CHRA and is the information dissemination arm of the Association and focuses on running an information drop-in centre for residents to air their views and acts as a resource centre for information dissemination and acquisition. Through the Information Blitz Project, CHRA convenes civic education workshops at grassroots level to empower residents on their rights. The Project is also used as a platform for disseminating various information packages for grassroots advocacy initiatives with the objective of developing a critical mass that will act as a bulwark against authoritarianism and in defence of democracy and transparent governance. Through this Project, CHRA is able to update the public and act as a public response to the poor service delivery crises in the capital as residents demand for quality municipal service and elections.

Other key activities of the Information Blitz Project include the administration of a drop-in centre through which the Association runs an information drop–in centre akin to a suggestion box in the Central Business District (CBD) in order to facilitate easy access to residents and where residents can contribute to debates or make representations on issues that affect them as residents and CHRA registered members. The drop-in centre receives complaints on issues such as City of Harare water and electricity bills, reports on the state of service delivery. Through the Project, CHRA is able to provide advice to residents on issues concerning city billing, as well as municipal and local governance issues in general. The Association also conducts civic education workshops where it tackles issues that concern citizens. The Association has also adopted drama and theatre as a mobilisation and information dissemination strategy where it established the tribunal concept set along the lines of a people's court, with the people being the final judges on the matter. The concept of making residents the final judges to mock trials figuratively portrays the pivotal role that citizens should play in the affairs of the city in general and decision-making processes both at local and central government levels. In the theatre which ensues, fictional characters hinged on real life persons will be put on trial, and there will have defence counsel and a people's prosecutor. The Association establishes the tribunal through the identification of community members who will constitute the judges, defence counsel and the people's prosecutor. Such programmes have enabled CHRA to create a fearless and sensitive constituency among its membership who are able to confront local authorities on issues that affect their lives.

The adoption of CHRA's militant strategy has been as a result of pressure from residents due to a spate of continued poor service delivery. Through mobilisation of residents, CHRA has been able to embark on popular campaigns which have usually been staged at both local levels with the communities in the City Centre. Popular campaigns remain the Associations broad strategy to put pressure on the local authority for the radical improvement in service provision and the restoration of good, transparent and accountable leadership at Town House. In addition to popular campaigns, CHRA has established healthy networks and alliances with various sectors of the civil society movement in order to promote a platform for receiving feedback, tapping new ideas and promoting the Association's ideas and strategies with the civic society. As part of advocacy, the Association holds networking meetings with other civil society organisations in a show of solidarity with the whole pro-democracy civil society movement in the country and beyond.

CHRA runs public meetings across most residential areas and the city centre. The meetings provide a platform for civic and human rights education as well as community mobilization platforms on the Association's campaigns. Mass publication and dissemination of information materials have also formed a vital publicity mechanism where the Association develops T-Shirts, and publishes publicity reading material such '*The Residents*' newsletter, pamphlets, fliers and DVD's for distributions to the wider membership, civic society organizations, government and stakeholder partners. In addition the project also facilitates weekly media monitoring updates and briefings, *sms* alerts on current developments, success story campaigns, website management, e-newsletter and press statements on key positions of the Association. These are success stories which CHRA has been able to formulate with a view to sharpening its strategies of mobilising residents on pertinent issues of governance.

CHRA in support of Democracy

Democratic discourse has been able to manifest itself through the Urban Councils Act (1996) which creates participatory spaces for citizens by empowering residents to form social associations such as residents associations whose propensity to democratise decision-making processes at local government is visible through the operations of these associations.

Subsequently, residents' associations portray a legal creation of the Urban Council Act [Chapter 29:15] which stipulates that residents are entitled to the formation of (an) association(s) that would help to address their concerns as ratepayers and to involve themselves in civic affairs and budgetary processes of the local government authority, thereby enhancing citizen participation in local governance. The Combined Harare Combined Residents' Association (CHRA) is one such creation. In other cities and towns, similar formations have been established and where there were no such social utilities, new ones are being created and defunct one resuscitated. Residents associations have not existed in a vacuum, especially in the mammoth task of fighting for democracy and the establishment of democratic structures in al spheres of government. As a result, the association has often worked with other members of the pro-democratic civil society movement in the country.

As marketing and commemoration strategy and a member of the international community, the Combined Harare Residents' Association has, on several occasions, joined the world in commemorating various significant ceremonies, especially the International Day For Democracy, which is commemorated very 15th day of September each year. This is in line with its vision which is *To be an effective watchdog and vehicle for good governance [in Harare] and as a model for advocacy*, a vision which is a significant pointer to its quest for a democratic dispensation in local governance in the country. In recent years, the International Day For Democracy has come at a time "when the nation of Zimbabwe is going through local and national governance crises that is a result of the failure by political leaders to observe the tenets of democracy"[3] and afford the

---

[3] CHRA and the quest for Democracy in Local Governance; Available on www.chra.org [Accessed 23 February 2009]

people of Zimbabwe free participatory spaces and freedom to partake in authentic electoral processes[4].

CHRA has, through various initiatives, maintained its space within the fight for democracy in Zimbabwe by engaging with sister residents' associations across the country in addition to other pro-democratic civic groupings in the country. This has been at various fora where the Association has advocated for good local governance and the participation of residents in local governance issues in Harare, and beyond. For residents' associations which were formed at the same time as CHRA, like in Bulawayo, the second capital city of the country, CHRA has been at the forefront of trading notes with the Progressive Bulawayo Residents Association (PBRA) and the Bulawayo United Residents Association (BURA), both of which have since merged to form the Progressive United Bulawayo Residents Association (PUBRA). CHRA has also been pivotal in capacitating other Residents' Associations like Chitungwiza Residents and Ratepayers' Association (CHIRRA), Masvingo United Residents and Ratepayers Association (MURRA) and others to fight for the same cause. In addition to capacitating existing residents associations, CHRA has also embarked on helping in the resuscitation of defunct old structures of residents associations which had since ceased to function in areas like Kwekwe, Shurugwi, Kadoma and Gweru. It has also been instrumental in the formation of new residents associations in smaller towns like Norton, Chinhoyi and Karoi. Plans are also underway to help setting up of similar structures in growth points, many of which have attained town status in recent years, like in Gokwe, Gutu, Chibi and Mwenezi.

Beyond the confines of Harare, CHRA has fought against the privatization of water services through the rejection of the Zimbabwe National Water Authority (ZINWA) takeover of water and sewer reticulation services from the City of Harare. It has even engaged the Ministry of Local Government to protest against moves to privatisation of water and reticulation services, arguing that in addition to being incapable of sustaining the mammoth task of water provision, the move would result in water becoming expensive and beyond the reach of many urban residents most of whom do not have a reliable source of income. Petitions, demonstrations and refusal to pay for water services by residents were a visible manifestation of the level of disenchantment that prevailed among

---

[4] Refer to the article **Mapuva, J** (2010) *"Militarization of Public Institutions, Flawed Electoral Processes and Citizen Participation"* in **Journal of Legislative Studies**, Volume 16, Number 4 (December 2010).

the residents. Elected councillors brought numerous presentations of protests before the state. As had been predicted by CHRA, the privatisation of water provision services had dare consequences for citizens, especially given the fact that the Zimbabwe National Water Authority (ZINWA), a government parastatal did not have the capacity to undertake and sustain the project, resulting in serious shortages of clean drinking water, with some urban areas having to go for weeks without water, further exposing citizens to disease outbreaks. The cholera outbreak that occurred in 2008 has been attributed to the suicidal and arbitrary decision by government to privatise water and reticulation services. Before the cholera outbreak, CHRA had on numerous occasions, warned of the possibility of such an outbreak and it was partly in the wake of this cholera outbreak which made the government to realise that it had made a grievous mistake and was forced to retract and return water provision to local authorities in all urban areas in the country. The government also realised that it should have sought public opinion from citizens on whether to privatise water and reticulation services of not.

Campaigns by CHRA and other residents associations across the country against continued privatisation of waters services resulted in the government discontinuing the provision of water and handing it back to local authorities as had been the case over the years. The Association believes that the signing of a Memorandum of Understanding between the Ministry of Water and Infrastructural Adjustment and the City of Harare where the City of Harare will resume its duties of delivering water to Harare residents is a result of the pressure that was put on the Ministry by the residents.

In addition to service delivery, CHRA has also been involved in local government electoral processes, arguing that it is the right of residents to choose and be served by officials that they choose. As a result CHRA has on numerous occasions made overtures and exhibited the commitment to engage the Minister of Local Government in a bid to force the Ministry of Local Government to conduct council and mayoral elections in Harare and remove the Commission[5] that was running the affairs of the city. The ousting of the Mudzuri-led Council ushered in a period when the affairs of the City of Harare were being managed by commissions that were not

---

[5] Harare was administered by a Commission after a constitutionally elected MDC-dominated Council was frustrated by the Minister of Local Government when the Mayor of Harare, Engineer Elias Mudzuri was removed by the Minister of Local Government, Dr Ignatious Chombo and accused of maladministration, a vague term which can imply anything abstract.

elected by Harare residents and did not represent the interests and priorities of residents. At the same time the Minister of Local Government arbitrarily dismissed elected councillors, resulting in residents refusing to recognise the caretaker Commission which was hand-picked by the Minister to administer the affairs of the City of Harare.

Above all, the Association has been fighting at a national level for local governance to be categorically enshrined within the constitution of Zimbabwe with no grey areas that the Minister would manipulate to disenfranchise residents. CHRA strongly feels that the Urban Councils Act (1996) should be enshrined within any new Constitution of Zimbabwe that may be coming after the constitution-making consultations so that if any amendments are to be made, the participation of residents will be ensured. Talking about the constitution of the country, CHRA has mobilised its members through its structures so that once citizens are given the opportunity to contribute to the constitution-making process, they would all express in unison the need to clip the wings of the Minister of Local Government and the constitution to provide for participatory budgetary processes to replace the current scenario where there is emphasis on *consultation* rather than *participation* in which local councils may decide to *consult* citizens at their own discretion since the local authorities are not obliged by the Urban Councils Act to incorporate citizens to *partake* in budgetary processes. The recent Local Government Laws Amendment Act that saw the office of the mayor being given a ceremonial status did not go down well with most residents in Harare and other different cities and towns as they felt that mayors should be given executive powers to effectively help in the formulation and implementation of developmental policies for their cities. In a democratic society in general and local government in particular, residents should be given the latitude to participate in the formulation of laws that govern them and their areas of residence. Moreover, the rights of residents deserve constitutional attention, not political attention. Local governance in Zimbabwe has been grossly infiltrated and influenced by central government, a situation which the Association felt was a threat to the tenets of democracy.CHRA has also shown interest in national electoral processes, and this is shown in its expression that it has been deeply saddened by the political violence that took place during the run-up to the June 27 2008 Presidential run-off elections which saw about 38 members of the Association being tortured for showing sympathy for different political parties, with more than 500 civil society members being murdered and many more displaced from their homes, both in urban and rural areas in politically-motivated violence[6]. CHRA has added its voice to the strong condemnation of violence of any nature, especially against those of its members and citizens of Zimbabwe who are perceived of having voted for the MDC during the March 2008 Harmonised Elections in which the MDC won. Members of CHRA believe that each citizen should be given the right to freely express their views and opinions without any fear of victimization or coercion. CHRA has also expressed acknowledgement to the electorate for having heeded the call to elect local leaders of their choice despite violence that accompanied the elections. CHRA also welcome the presence of the new council (mainly composed of members of the MDC) which they believe will go a long way in ensuring that Harare will be restored to its former status of being the Sunshine City through quality service delivery.The Association has since generated capacity building programmes that are aimed at boosting the capacity of the newly-elected councillors in tackling local governance challenges. Meanwhile CHRA has led the residents of Harare, through CHRA information dissemination mechanisms in reminding all stakeholders to the Inter-Party dialogue that they will not agree to any settlement, political or otherwise, that threatens democracy or compromises the tenets of good local governance in Zimbabwe such as *accountability*, *transparency* and *participation*. The Association has exhorted other residents associations across the country to emulate the same. Harare residents have also vowed to ensure that democracy is promoted in Zimbabwe through the establishment of systems and procedures that promote the maximum participation of the ordinary citizen in local governance issues. CHRA has further approached and communicated the message that the Southern Africa Development Community (SADC), the African Union (AU) and the United Nations (UN) must critically work with the Zimbabwean citizens to put an end to the eco-political crisis that the nation has faced for the last two decades. The Association will again continue to join hands with all progressive forces in ensuring that democracy is promoted within local governance and at national level.

Mobilisation, Engagement and Networking

In terms of what Tilly (in Bantjes, 2007) calls "social movement repertoire" CHRA's activities have become increasingly typical of

---

[6] Zimbabwe Human Rights NGO Forum *"The burden of politics on women in Zimbabwe"*. Available on http://www.hrforumzim.com/press/Politically_Motivated_Violence.htm

ordinary social movement organisations which are indicative of contentious politics that the organisation has adopted since the turn of the century, particularly after the arbitrary expulsion of the popularly elected executive mayor and council and their subsequent replacement by a government-appointed commission in 2004 (Kamete, 2009:63). In the context of Zimbabwe's socio-political and economic environment, public meetings and challenging violations of the Urban Councils Act and other legislation can hardly be non-contentious, especially considering that the state is being increasingly characterized as repressive and intolerant (Kamete, 2009:63). Given this environment, coupled with increasingly poor service delivery and perennial sewerage bursts, it come as no surprise that CHRA has adopted a more confrontational attitude in their demand for improved service delivery and accountability, both of which are dependent on good governance[7].

While CHRA's historical mandate has remained the same, its thrust and strategies have changed, and is now characterized by direct confrontation with the state.It has expressed its sensitivity to residents' plight of increasingly poor service delivery, which has resulted in recently years in the outbreak of the cholera pandemic and other associated ailments. CHRA's attitude towards the state has been modelled by the state's confrontational and uncompromising attitude, its perceived insensitivity to residents' petitions and its undemocratic governance practices in the cities, all of which have made constructive dialogue and engagement difficult, if not impossible (Kamete, 2009:63). Kamete (2009:64) further notes that the state's politicization of every form of dissent and disagreement, where all those who question government decisions and make demands are lumped together with the political opposition, as well as militarising various public institutions[8] have both played a significant role in radicalizing the movement.

The increasingly hostile and beleaguered state necessitated CHRA to undergo a paradigm shift in its mobilization strategies. The shift in engaging the state has been complemented by a shift in mobilizing its members and casting its net wider to incorporate those that had previously been excluded. While previously, its attention was on the middle and high-income property owners, CHRA has now expanded its constituency to

---

[7] Op.Cit

[8] Refer to Mapuva, J (2010) "*Militarization of Public Institutions, Flawed Electoral Processes and Citizen Participation*" in *Journal of Legislative Studies*, Volume 16, Number 4 (December 2010).

include those in the low-income bracket (Kamete, 2009, unpublished paper). Research has shown that such groups of people, who by virtue of their deprivation, are easy to mobilize in demand for improved service delivery. On the same note, Burrows & Loader (2007:345) argue that the nature of political institutions is transformed with a limited scope for local democracy and changes originating from the centre. Kamete (2009:65) has noted that one reason why the state in Zimbabwe has taken note of CHRA and responded to its criticism is because the Association has reached deep into the low-income areas where disenchantment is more prevalent. In fact, state repression over the years, coupled with the economic crisis may be partly responsible for increasing CHRA membership since 2000, given the emergence of high poverty levels especially in urban areas, shortage of basic commodities and appalling service delivery.

For a long time CHRA has operated in a repressive political and unstable economic environment that has plunged the country into a series of multiple crises since the early 2000s, all of which have been a result of a crisis of governance. It has been argued that the many and varied socio-political and economic tribulations that have be-devilled the country since 2000 are a result of a crisis of governance (Chikuhwa,2004:256 in Kamete, 2009), the spin-offs of which impacted negatively on residents who had to contend with corruption, poor service delivery and shortages of basic commodities. This resulted in residents losing faith in public institutions which have become heavily politicised, with key ministries such as those of the Ministry of Local Government, Public Works and Urban Development, as well as the Zimbabwe Republic Police having become extensions of ZANU PF. Of particular relevance to CHRA's operations has been the ZANU PF government's repressive infrastructure, particularly legislation restricting the rights of citizens such as the freedom of expression, association and assembly, which CHRA has criticised as"…costly, flawed and frustrating…"(CHRA, 2006b). In attempting to *"call tyranny to account"*, CHRA has taken a number of steps which according to Kamete (2007) has been necessitated by the despotic and politicisation (and in some cases, militarization) of local governance in Zimbabwe. These included contesting the legitimacy of imposed authority by the Ministry of Local Government and Urban Development in an MDC-dominated local authority; challenging the legitimacy of the Commission which had been so imposed by the Minster of Local Government after the ouster of the democratically elected Mayor of Harare, one Engineer Elias Mudzuri, now the Minister of Energy in the Inclusive Government. CHRA has also shown its commitment to citizen participation by claiming spaces for citizens in budgetary processes (CHRA, 2006b) in the Harare City Council. Thirdly, CHRA has sought to be consulted by the Ministry of Local Government in matters that affect the livelihood of residents and ratepayers by contesting government's arbitrary decision-making processes, with the transfer of water and sewerage services to a parastatal, the Zimbabwe National Water Authority (ZINWA). Calling for the takeover to be annulled, CHRA argued that the move "...further exposes the evil agenda of the regime towards urban citizens, particularly those living in Harare..."(CHRA, 2006b). The association has associated the alienation of CHRA by the former ZANU PF government as a vindication for showing support for the MDC in all elections. The statement captures CHRA's modus operandi which is activated through litigation, advocacy, disruption and information campaigns (Kamete, 2009:69).

CHRA in collaborative with other Civil Society Organizations

Civil society groups in Zimbabwe have over the years, adopted a trend of collaborating or forming coalitions, alliances or *ad hoc* unions in an effort to strengthen their voices of dissent over pertinent issues of governance such as human rights, electoral processes and even the repulsion of restrictive legislation. Those sections of the pro-democratic movement that CHRA has been in league with includes those from the ecumenical sector, the labour and student movements among others. All these sections of civil society have been pulled together by their common desire to reclaim democratic space and campaign together for the restoration of democracy in the country and the reinstating of democratic institutions in various sectors in the country.

The diminishing of democratic spaces in recent years has tended to pull different civic groups, initially with divergent views, closer together to buttress their demand for the restoration of democracy in the country. Even religious groups which have been known for solely embarking on ecumenical work unless in catastrophic cases and gross human rights violations, have been involved in the demand for the restoration of democracy. One such religious grouping, the Catholic Commission for Justice and Peace (CCJP) has spearheaded an investigation into human rights violation during the Matabeleland Massacres of the 1980s where according to its findings, more than 20 000 people were killed, and many more displaced[9]. Another religious coalition, Christian Alliance also formed around the notion of the promotion of human rights transcended religious boundaries and attempted to voice their concern for disregard of the rule of law, gross human rights and increasing poverty among the general populace in the country. The Alliance was an *ad hoc* association of like-minded pro-democratic Christian leaders in Zimbabwe who feel called by God to be instrumental in resolving Zimbabwe's political and economic crises through non-violent means or peaceful advocacy processes for the benefit of the Zimbabwean people. Its objectives include building a critical mass of public opinion on issues of justice and peace; to take a prophetic Christian stance with boldness in proclamation and action; mobilize regional and international solidarity and pressure; and to contribute towards the development of a new democratic constitution (Christian Alliance, 2007). The Christian Alliance at its inception revealed that it is not a political formation, nor does it harbour political ambitions, but has the objective of calling upon the establishment to address issues of concern to the public and ensure that citizen rights are protected and promoted. They call for good and accountable governance by all leadership regardless of their political allegiance.

Another rallying point for civil society desperate to have human rights violation curtailed through engagement with the bureaucracy, was the Broad Alliance, formed along the same mode as the Christian Alliance. In a desperate move to strengthen their position as a viable pro-democratic force, civic organizations of different persuasions, have rallied behind either a loose coalition, such as the Broad Alliance formed to express concerns for human rights violation in early 2002, or strong coalitions such as the NCA with a specific objective of constitutional reform. The formation of the Broad Alliance is an indication that a wide spectrum of the Zimbabwean people has the desire to elect their own government (Africa Report, No 93). Either way, civil society organizations have realized the need for a collaborative approach and concerted effort to restore democracy in Zimbabwe because the magnitude of the problem of diminishing democratic spaces could only be addressed through a collaborative approach by civil society and the state (Candler, 2005:248).

CHRA has also collaborated with other pro-democratic civic groups to strengthen citizen participation. In an effort to strengthen their position in

---

[9] CCJP and LRF (1996) *"Breaking the Silence Report on the Disturbances in Matabeleland and the Midlands"* 'Gukurahundi in Zimbabwe; Jacana Publishers

the fight for democracy, CHRA has forged working relationships and established linkages with other pro-democratic forces in the country, notably the Zimbabwe Congress of Trade Unions (ZCTU), Zimbabwe's biggest labour union as well as the country's biggest political pressure group, the National Constitution Assembly (NCA), which is a coalition of over 250 civil society groups comprising churches, civic and human rights groups, women's organizations, the Zimbabwe National Students' Union (ZINASU), the main student movement as well as other civic groups. On many occasions, CHRA has joined these and other civil society groups in calling for good governance and the establishment of a democratic dispensation in the country. In conjunction with the ZCTU, ZINASU and the NCA, CHRA regularly joined in the call for an indefinite strike by workers to press for the establishment of a transitional authority to draw up a new constitution for the country that will lead to free and fair elections. These civic groups have, on several occasions, met to "plot their push for transitional government in Zimbabwe saying only such an authority would be best equipped to break the country's long-running political crisis" (Spectrum, 2009). Various players in civil society movement in Zimbabwe have shown resentment to the power-sharing arrangement between the ruling ZANU PF and opposition MDC parties, arguing that ZANU PF, in power for almost 30 years, does not have anything new to offer the people of Zimbabwe and has even been blamed for the deterioration of the economy and the destruction of the agricultural sector through the chaotic land redistribution exercise which eventually disrupted the commercial sector. Additionally CHRA and other pro-democratic forces in the country have argued that election results in 2008 indicated that ZANU PF is no more fit to rule and as such should relinquish power to the winning MDC without recourse to a GNU formation.

Chapter Five

CHRA and the Participatory Budgetary Process

In theory many countries provide for some form of consultation or participation during the budget process. This is to enable citizens to make contributions (input or objections) to the local authority. This has usually occurred mainly at the beginning of the process and in only a few countries is public input solicited after the final budget has been put together. Although the budget process allows for consultation and/or participation, it is not always clear that input from citizens is taken seriously. In many cases the budget still appears to be driven by officials and to lesser extent councillors although it a by way of formality that the budget is gazetted or flighted in the media for citizens to respond. However, officials are well aware that many citizens (especially those in high density) do not bother to consult newspapers for such budgets, preferring to spend their time on fending for their families. To the ordinary citizens the budget figures as they appear in the media is meaningless and appear to be a list of financial statements or figures.

Local government in Zimbabwe is governed by the Urban Councils Act and the Rural District Councils Act. In addition to carrying out the functions and powers detailed in these acts, local authorities can make policy through bylaws, regulations, and resolutions dealing with local planning and development. This translates to the fact that local government authorities have the power to manage their own fiscal revenues and expenditures, subject to national framework conditions and can thus be viewed as semi-autonomous. Bylaws of councils cannot, however, become law unless the Minister of local Government approves them as such. Given the wide ranging powers that the Minister of Local Government holds in Zimbabwe, one is confident that the Minister as a politician falls victims to the whims of corrupt politicians who would not allow such powers to be usurped through allowing citizens to participate in the decision-making processes of local authorities in the country. This is one of the challenges that the CHRA has had to contend to, where the

Minister of Local Government is a ZANU PF apologist and given that most of the elected officials in many urban areas belong to the Movement for Democratic Change while the Minister is from ZANU PF. Consequently, the Minister of Local Government has continued to frustrate efforts of elected councillors and the CHRA to work with the Harare City Council to resolve issues of service delivery fearing that the successes scored by the MDC-dominated local authorities would call for comparisons between the performance of the two political parties where ZANU PF councillors have been portrayed as not only corrupt but incompetent.

Local government in Zimbabwe uses a variety of instruments for public consultation. These include the government gazette; notices calling for objections in more than one issue of the newspaper; public notices at the local authorities' offices; ministerial commissions; ministerial investigations; consultation with local authority; councillor input; ward development committees; the right of the community to attend council meetings; the right of citizens to make copies of bylaws, budgets, resolutions, and voter rolls; and council subcommittees. According to Shall in World Bank (2007:204) "[T]hese mechanisms assume a high degree of literacy and interest in civic matters on the part of citizens and are consistent with a top-down approach" which makes them practically accessible to the general rate payers. Working on these assumptions does not reflect the situation on the ground because not all citizens are privileged enough to have access to most of the cited sources of information nor are they all that literate as well as assuming that most of the citizens are that interested in civic matters unless during a time of crisis such as during gross human rights violations or in an era of bad governance. Although Zimbabwe may be credited with a high literacy rate, it appears that these mechanisms are not as widely used as initially envisaged or as it may appear on paper. Considerations should be put to the fact that many citizens are more concerned with immediate bread-and-butter issues and in most cases do not spare time to politicking.

Additionally, the current Constitution of Zimbabwe which has been in use for almost three decades does not make detailed provisions for local government and the only enabling legislation, the Urban Councils Act advocates for consultation rather than participation, which means that local authorities are not compelled to incorporate residents but may consult them on issues that they think are necessary to do so. This puts residents at the mercy of local authorities which, constitutionally, are empowered to make decisions for and on behalf of residents. In Zimbabwe, Uganda,

Kenya and Ethiopia local government legislation is such that citizens are not included in the decision-making process "...but are permitted to make public objections after decisions have been made" (World Bank, 2007:195) by technocrats in municipalities. This makes a mockery of the citizens who, in the first instance, are the very people from whose payments the local authority thrives.

However, there have been attempts by the Urban and Rural Councils Act to adopt a grassroots approach, beginning with development committees in each branch/village, district and provincial levels, usually chaired by a local councillor and this has attempted to bring decision-making issues to the door step of every citizen. The main function of these development committees is "...to prepare and submit an annual development plan to the local councillor/s who would then make recommendations to a full council meeting attended by council officials so that such plans can be incorporated into the annual and long-term development plans of the city or town (World Bank, 2007:205).

Given this window of opportunity created by such interactions, and despite various non-committal nature of existing legislation, CHRA has made attempts to approach the Harare City Council to have input from residents incorporated into the financial budgets of the City of Harare through the use of local councillors. CHRA has also made use of a number of mobilizing strategies to draw the attention of the local authorities of rate payers' grievances. Additionally, CHRA has employed various mobilization strategies and modes of engagement in its engagement with the city council on behalf of rate payers in particular and residents in general including through making presentations to the local authority and in press reports. CHRA has canvassed for public participation in budgetary processes within the City of Harare through its Advocacy Centre and the drop-in-centres where citizens can share with CHRA officials on what they want to see being done to incorporate residents in the affairs of the local authority. Under a press statement entitled *"CHRA objects to Council's proposal to borrow*[1]*"* CHRA berated the Combined Harare City Council for extravagance at a time when ratepayers were riling under abject poverty and poor service delivery, with threatening conditions of uncollected refuse and burst sewer pipes exposing residents to a disease outbreak.

---

[1] CHRA objects to Council's proposal to borrow"zimbabwesituation.com. ONLNE publication -z25 September 2009

Chapter Five

CHRA has also demanded accountability on expenditure and income from the City Council Treasury Department. It has come out strongly against the Harare City Council's skewed priorities and demanded that it should be consulted before the Council embarks on projects and purchases of utilities. In its public statement, the Combined Harare Residents' Association (CHRA) has registered its objection to the City of Harare's arbitrary expenditure without recourse to public views and participation with the local authority's resolution to borrow US$150 000 to service the water channelling and sewer reticulation pipes[2]. CHRA is of the view that such borrowings should have the blessing of the rate payers whose rental and rates are used to service such a debt. The decision to object to this resolution is informed by the poor prioritization of service delivery issues that have been displayed by the City Council in the past. Recently the City Council has spent over USD300 000 on purchasing 3 luxury vehicles for the Mayor and two directors at the expense of attending to the poor health facilities within the city. CHRA reiterates that it is not the position of the Association that the council (currently with many projects waiting) must not buy vehicles for the Mayor and its workers. However, the Association makes it categorically clear that it was unnecessary and an act of extravagant expenditure for the council to buy such expensive vehicles at a time when service delivery is at its lowest ebb in the city. The Mayor's car cost USD153 000 while the two Directors' cars cost USD90 000 each, a fortune in Zimbabwean standards and an amount that a can be put to better use that can be beneficial to the generality of residents of Harare. The Association is of the view that such money could have been used to service the water and sewer pipes as well as procure water treatment chemicals. CHRA also calls on the council to satisfactorily account for the revenue collected from the residents so far, before the council decides to borrow from anywhere, and to revel how the debt will be serviced and whether the debt will bring about an increase in the rates paid by residents. CHRA has since [and in many similar instances] written to the Mayor expressing its objection to the idea of borrowing this [and various arbitrary] resolution[s]. The Association has also mobilised residents and its members to submit letters of objection addressed to the Town Clerk through the association's drop-in points. As a facilitative measure, CHRA has made provisions for their members and residents to approach the CHRA offices for assistance in this regard. CHRA has since developed a standardized objection letter which residents and members can complete

---

[2] "CHRA objects to Council's proposal to borrow" ONLINE publication [25 September 2009]

for submission to the Town Clerk. This shows that CHRA remains steadfast and resolved in lobbying for accountability and transparency in local governance in the City of Harare and has even influenced other cities across the country to act the same and has offered to provide the logistics and expertise to equip other residents associations to establish infrastructure for engagement with city and town councils within their respective constituencies throughout the country.

The Role of Councillors as Elected Officials

The role of councillors as elected officials has come into the spotlight following questions about their role in council. There has been a quagmire among councillors as role conflict characterizes their operations and functionalities. It has emerged that there is a clash of interest which tends to place councillors in a quagmire as they are forced to place their allegiance to both residents and council simultaneously. What has further exacerbated the quagmire has been the fact that while they may purport to represent local resident who will have elected them into office, they constitute the decision-making machinery of the local authority and in most cases, dispense decisions which impinge on residents' rights and freedoms. They have ended up not knowing whether to serve and represent residents who elected them into office and as council officials whose mandate would be to make policy with the local governance framework. The role conflict comes when councillors as elected officials and council ex-officios, are required to act as the voice of residents and at the same time are required to enforce council resolutions some of which are very punitive, especially council resolutions that pertain to residents who default in their payments of council dues.

Discussions that ensued between the author and councillors presented a quagmire as to their role and allegiance in their operations. While in council, it emerged that the councillors form part of the policy-making body, some policies of which infringe residents' rights. As elected officials, councillors partake in the budgetary process of the local authority on behalf of residents, a move rejected by CHRA which argued that these officials are in council not as representatives of residents but as an policy-making machinery of the local authority and as such should not purport to stand in for residents. An example of a council resolution which Council reached which infringes residents' rights is where all those residents who are unable to settle their dues will have their water meters or electricity disconnected. This presented councillors with a precarious situation where as elected officials, they should have been seen working for the good of the residents and not making life difficult for them. Some councillors even confessed that they are equally confused as to whether they represent residents in council or they are being used to make resolutions which would injure not only the residents, but their standing and integrity as elected officials who will seek re-election at some stage from the same residents.

What also emerged from informal discussions with councillors was that the fact that councillors are elected on political party lines resulted in them viewing each other with suspicion with some of them using the platform to project objectives of their respective political parties. This has tended to create lack of synergy in council debates as each political party represented herein attempts to gain political mileage by trying to outwit other political parties. This tug-of-war has also created disunity and disharmony. A councillor expressed the view that this lack of synergy was being caused by councillors from ZANU PF who have tasted power for many years and as such, are not able to contend with playing second fiddle to the MDC councillors who are a majority not only in Harare but in all local authorities (urban and rural) across the country. Consequently, the author observed that this lack of synergy has impacted negatively on residents as it impedes on residents' propensity to participate in local governance.

However, the issue of role conflict on the part of councillors was vehemently shot down by Dr Randal Smith, one of my chief respondents, a local government consultant, and a specialist in local governance and working within a local government environment in East London, who argued that councillors should be guided by their citizenship conviction and sense of responsibility more than by their personal instincts or political affiliation and survival. Dr Randal Smith further argued that residents as responsible citizens have a duty and responsibility to ensure that local authority functions and that payment of dues to municipality is part of their responsibility. As such putting aside issues of politics, measures to enforce compliance by council are necessary. He further noted that once councillors are elected into council they also have a duty and responsibility "to make decisions and enforce them". Dr Randal Smith concurred with the idea of taking enforcement measures to ensure that residents comply with council decisions, some decisions which might seem punitive. He expressed the notion that cities and towns should not be allowed to degenerate into ungovernable entities with dilapidated infrastructure due to reneging residents and as such the enforcement of laws and bylaws to curtail disobedience and non-compliance should be upheld. However, he pointed out that there has got to be dialogue between residents and the local authority on how residents should comply and within a given time frame. O'Neill (2008) has pointed out that "a personally responsible citizen is 'good' in the sense of being law abiding and responsible and ….exhibits elements of social citizenship and responsibility". The respondent further noted that both councillors and residents should exhibit elements of citizenship, responsibility, and accountability should be prepared to be called to account on issues that are their realm of responsibility.

Chapter Six

Interpretation and Implications of CHRA's Activities

The activities of CHRA have presented the association with an opportunity to speak on behalf of residents of Harare and its environs. It has been able to do this through effective mobilisation strategies and has been helped in its endeavours by the deteriorating standards of living and appalling service delivery standards. Consequently residents have come to identify with the objectives of the association which they have come to regard as sympathetic with their plight.

CHRA's activities and thrust falls into the realms of a social movement and as such finds itself unconsciously entangled into the trap of being in politics of the country without realising it. CHRA's mandate, crusade and tactics have raised questions about social movements in general and those operating in repressive environments in particular. Chester and Welsh (2010) note that social movements find it difficult to ensure good [local] governance without being tainted by projects of regime change and in this case, CHRA has been swept with the same brush. On its position of endeavouring to influence the establishment of good local governance, and even on national governance, CHRA has pointed out that it has "…been forced by the regime's hegemonic and exclusivist policies to address questions of national politics…until changes [of involving residents in the decision-making processes] occur that will allow [CHRA] to operate normally as a social movement (McAdam, McCarthy and Zald, 2006:10 in Kamete, 2007). The authors further note that there could be no clearer admission of complicity in a regime change agenda, and as such they acknowledge that "…part of the move towards a more democratic dispensation in Zimbabwe, CHRA's stance clearly resonates with proponent of democratic (regime) change" (McAdam, McCarthy &Zald, 2006:10). However, what distinguishes CHRA as a social movement from an interest group is that "…interest groups are seen as self-interested, that is, organizations established to pursue the self-interests of their members (Candler, 1999:239), while social movements like CHRA"…are seen as positive, democratizing players in public polity" which makes CHRA straddle between the two definitions. While protecting the interests of residents has been its initial mandate, CHRA has consistently transcended this confinement by calling on central government to account on broader issues of government and governance, thereby playing a dual role as a social movement and interest group (Allen, 2007 in Kamete,2009).

As part of its fight against corruption and lawlessness that is aimed at intimidating the general citizenry, CHRA has adopted an aggressive strategy of demanding that the law takes its course on unruly behaviour by those perpetuating politically-motivated violence. A case in point is when CHRA demanded that the ZANU PF Member of Parliament for Harare, one Honourable Hubert Nyanhongo be arrested and arraigned before the courts of law to answer to charges of motivating violence to residents belonging to other political parties and corruption in the allocation of market stalls in the capital city in favour of ZANU PF supporters, all at the expense of the poor residents of Harare who desperately need these to augment their meagre salaries or as the sole source of survival. The newspaper article read in part:

> The Combined Harare Residents Association (CHRA) has since written to Officer Commanding Harare Central police station requesting the arrest of Hon. Nyanhongo for inciting public violence and disorder. Hon Nyanhongo issued out statements to the press threatening the city council and residents who will benefit from the re allocation of the market stalls. Kindly find attached the letter that was written to the Officer Commanding Harare Central Police Station.[1]

This is one of the most daring acts that CHRA has embarked on, and portrays the tenets of a social movement whose activities are very unusual and with daring consequences.

Despite a repressive and hostile environment, coupled with an unstable economic environment, which plunged the country into a series of multiple crises since the early 2000s, all of which have been a result of a crisis of governance, CHRA has defied all odds by criticising the bureaucracy at a time when doing so was suicidal. It has been argued that the many and varied socio-political and economic tribulations that have bedevilled the country since 2000 are a result of a crisis of governance,

---

[1] "CHRA demands the arrest of Hon. Nyanhongo" CHRA Press statement, 21 September 2009; Available on
http://www.zimbabwesituation.com/sep22_2009.html [Accessed on 22 September 2009]

Chikuhwa (2004:256), whose spin-offs impacted negatively on residents who had to contend with corruption, poor service delivery and shortages of basic commodities. Militarisation and politicisation of numerous arms of government and institutions have led to citizens losing faith in the ZANU PF government, and among civil society organisations that have dared to criticise this arrangement was CHRA whose representation of residents translated to that of citizens on a national scale. Among public institutions that residents bemoaned as a result of politicisation and militarisation include those of key ministries such as those of the Ministry of Local Government, Public Works and Urban Development, as well as the Zimbabwe Republic Police having become extensions of ZANU PF. Of particular relevance to CHRA's operations has been the ZANU PF government's repressive infrastructure, particularly legislation restricting the freedom of freedom and assembly, which CHRA has criticised as"…costly, flawed and frustrating…" (CHRA, 2006b). In attempting to *"call tyranny to account"*, CHRA has taken a number of steps. These included contesting the legitimacy of imposed authority by the Ministry of Local Government and Urban Development in an MDC-dominated local authority; challenging the legitimacy of the Commission which had been so imposed by the Minster of Local Government after the latter has ousted the democratically elected Mayor of Harare, one Engineer Elias Mudzuri, now the Minister of energy in the Inclusive Government. CHRA has also shown its commitment for citizen participation by claiming spaces for citizens in budgetary processes (CHRA, 2006b) by the Harare City Council. Thirdly, CHRA has sought to be consulted by the Ministry of Local Government in matters that affect the livelihood of residents and ratepayers by contesting government's arbitrary decision-making processes, with the transfer of water and sewerage services to a parastatal, the Zimbabwe National Water Authority (ZINWA). Calling for the takeover to be annulled, CHRA argued that the move "…further exposes the evil agenda of the regime towards urban citizens, particularly those living in Harare…" (CHRA, 2006b).

CHRA has also been behind the consolidation of existing residents association, resuscitation and rejuvenation of those in limbo and the formation of similar local institutions in different towns and cities across the country. This is because CHRA has been a model for other similar-minded urban centres to emulate hence its influence to other urban areas has been magnanimous. CHRA's influence to other towns and cities has necessitated the resuscitation of defunct civic institutions that had long been forgotten, especially those that had existed during the colonial era as a bulwark against colonialism.

Due to increased awareness in civic affairs and the rights of citizens to influence local and central government decision-making processes, the author realized the resuscitation of once forgotten civic institutions like residents associations in smaller towns and cities. In Kwekwe, Kadoma, Kariba, Chegutu and a host of other cities and towns, there has been efforts to reinstate and reinstitute the once local defunct civic organs by making overtures to have residents influence local government policy within their cities and towns. In some cases, cities and towns like Gweru and Shurugwi are building on old resident association structures which had degenerated into obscurity due to non-functioning. Bigger cities like Harare and Bulawayo which had had splinter residents associations have strengthened these by combining these splinter associations into bigger ones, such as the Combined Harare Residents Association (CHRA) and the Bulawayo United Resident Association (BURA) in an effort to be able to tackle increasingly sophisticated issues of governance. The residents associations utilize participatory approaches to engagement with their members. Many of these associations which had all along operated on virtual basis are establishing offices and centres where residents can come for consultation.

CHAPTER SEVEN

CHALLENGES ENCOUNTERED AND LESSONS LEARNT IN IMPLEMENTING PARTICIPATORY BUDGETING

CHRA has encountered numerous challenges in its attempts to implement participatory budgeting. These challenges can be divided into technical as well as political and social challenges.

7.1 Technical Challenges

Participatory budgeting may have met with some successes in many parts of Africa, but challenges remain. CHRA have encountered numerous challenges in trying to be incorporated into the budgetary processes of local government, especially through some of their councillors. Councillors who are local people best positioned to form a link between the ratepayers (citizens) and the local authorities are the most serious impediment to civic participation in planning and budgeting. Given that CHRA comprises residents from low-income groups, most likely with low literacy levels, it is such citizens that are often not aware of their rights to participate, and they lack an understanding and awareness of policy-making and budgetary processes. Citizens are often not aware of their rights to participate, and they lack an understanding and awareness of policy-making and budgetary processes. This is exacerbated by the low literacy levels of most of these councillors. Generally, low level of literacy hampers participation. As a result citizens with very low levels of education tend to participate less, because they lack access to information and do not understand municipal procedures (World Bank, 2007:217). As a result, the budget-making process involves mainly the elite, especially given that the language used in discussing policy and budgets is often technical and introduces unfamiliar concepts which is beyond the comprehension of both councillors, the representatives of CHRA as well as any citizens who might to follow the budgetary process or make an input. This discourages them from further deliberations and attendance.

Councillors themselves lack adequate training to be able to impart the right information to residents on council activities and future projects whose implementation would need commitment of more funding from the rate payers themselves.

7.2 Political and economic challenges

Besides technical problems, CHRA has also encountered political and social problems over the last two decades, especially given that the country was experiencing political and economic crises. On the overall, CHRA has confessed that due to the hostility and militant characteristic of the ZANU PF government over the years, coupled with the enactment of restrictive legislation towards civil society and human rights activists, "there has not been much in terms of practical gains to ordinary Harare citizens, especially given the intransigence of the [Mugabe's] regime" (Kamete, 2007:71). CHRA qualifies this assertion by arguing that the situation has been exacerbated by the fact that the [ZANU PF] government has not heeded court rulings to empower ratepayers by upholding their choice of mayor[1] (CHRA, 2005). But on the other front, CHRA has argued that evidence suggests that non-payment is largely attributable to CHRA's strategy" of exhorting ratepayers to boycott payment of rates[2].

CHRA's activism is viewed by government as result of "oppositional forces bent on illegal regime change. Coincidentally, the presence of prominent CHRA personnel on sites of oppositional politics, such as demonstrations, is summarily linked to a partisan political project by the state. This has landed CHRA in a precarious position with the state such that any form of protest action would be attributed to the influence of opposition politics. However, on the whole the impact on CHRA's activism and its propensity to influence ratepayers in particular and the general citizenry has been encouraging and in some cases, has been able to influence policy, such as the need to officially install councillors who had been elected on a popular vote by citizens, which action was eventually done by the resistant Minister of Local Government and Urban Development.

---

[1] This was in reference to popularly-elected MDC Mayor of Harare, Engineer Elias Mudzuri who was dismissed by the Minister of Local Government, Dr Ignatious Chombo for "maladministration", and was replaced by a Commission that was arbitrarily appointed by the same Minister

[2] Mile Davies, CHRA chairperson, personal communication, 2 June 2008

Conclusion

The Combined Harare Residents Association has developed from an ordinary ratepayers' association to a vibrant more encompassing residents association grouping whose operations has displayed all the trappings of a social movement. CHRA has also developed from demanding for improved service delivery within its catchment area of Harare to assuming national issues such as curbing inflation and mobilising residents to participate in the constitution-making process. It has managed to mobilise its members not only to compel city authorities to address issues of service delivery and engage in civil disobedience, but has also called political authorities to account on national issues such as inflation, use of foreign currency to pay for services, especially at a time when workers were being paid in local currency. It has also demanded that political authorities put in place modalities for the drafting of a national constitution for the country.

In addition, CHRA has been able to influence developments and events within the Harare City Council through demanding residents' participation not only in budgetary processes, but in other decision-making processes that demand concerted efforts of the whole constituency. CHRA's impressive record of engaging the local authority and central government has impressed residents of other town and cities to the extent that others began to form similar institutions while those which had become defunct were resuscitated as the need to represent and participate in local governance became increasingly evident due to poor service delivery and rates and rents hikes which residents questioned regularly.

The participatory stance that CHRA has adopted through its structures shows that while it campaigns for participatory spaces from both local and central authorities, it is itself democracy, thereby leading by example. It is unlike many civic groups which demand participatory spaces from the authorities yet they are not democratic in their activities and behaviour. It has also come to the notice and attention of the author that many civic groups are run like personal fiefdoms by those in-charges of them.

REFERENCES

Bantjes.R (2007) Social Movements in a Global Context, CSPI

Barnes,M (1999). 'Users as citizens: collective action and the local governance of welfare' *Social Policy and Administration*, Vol.33, and No.1:73-90

Barnes,M and Skelcher,C (2007). Designing citizen-centred governance; California Joseph Rowntree Foundation

Bossuyt, Jean. Involving Non-State Actors and Local Governments in ACP-EU Dialogue (European, 2000)

Burrows, W &Loader, I. (2000) Plural Policing and Democratic Governance. *Social & Legal Studies* 9(3),323-45

Candler, G.G (2005) "Civil Society and Development: Scientific and Professional Associations in Public Policy in Santa Catarina and Sergipe, Brazil" *Policy Studies Journal*, 27(3)427-445

Chester, G &Welsh, I (eds)(2010). Introducing Social Movements, London, Amazon Books

CHRA (2009) "CHRA demands the arrest of Hon. Nyanhongo" CHRA Press statement, 21 September 2009; Available on http://www.zimbabwesituation.com/sep22_2009.html [Accessed on 19 October 2009]

Cohen, J and Fung, A (2001) 'Deepening democracy: Innovations in empowered participatory governance', *Politics and Society*, Vol 29 No 1: 5-41

Cohen, Joshua and Archon Fung. "Radical Democracy" in *Swiss Journal of Political Science* Vol. 10, No. 4 (2004 European Charter of Local Self-Government. CETS No.: 122

Gaventa, J, 2003a, 'Perspectives on Participation', paper presented at symposium *Developing Participation: Challenges for Policy and Practice*, Stockholm

—. 2003, 'Towards Participatory Governance: Assessing the Transformative Possibilities, paper presented at conference *Participation: From Tyranny to Transformation*, Manchester

Heyden, G. No Shortcuts to Progress: African Development Management in Perspective (Heinemann Publishers,1983)

Hyden, G and Braton, M (eds) (1993): Governance and Politics in Africa, Lynne Rienner, Boulder, Colorado

Jones, P. and Weale, A. 1999. *Democracy,* Palgrave, New York.

References

Kathlene, M & Martin, F (1991) "The Question of Participation: Toward Authentic Public Participation in Public Administration" *Public Administration Review,* Vol. 58, 1991

Kamete, A (2009) "For enhanced civic participation in local governance": calling tyranny to account in Harare" *Environment and Urbanization,* Vol. 21, No. 1, 59-75

Lwanga-Ntale, Golooba-Mutebi and Awoori Taaka. Civic Participation in Municipal Governance: The Case of Uganda, A Case Study prepared for Municipal Development Programme, 1999

Mafeje, A., "Theory of Democracy and the African discourse" in E.Chole and J. Ibrahim (eds), Democratization Processes in Africa: Problems and Prospects. CODESRIA Book Series,Dakar, 1995

Makumbe, J. (1996). Participatory Development: The Case of Zimbabwe, Human Rights Bulletin, March 1996, pp.21-25.

—. (1998), 'Is there a civil society in Africa?' *International Affairs* 74,(2);305-317

Mamadou, D. (1996) Africa's Management in the 1990's and beyond; Reconciling Indigenous and Transplanted Institutions: Washington: IBRD/The World Bank

Manor, J. (1999). The Political Economy of Democratic Decentralization. Washington, DC: World Bank.

O'Neill, B (2008) "Assessing the 'Education' in Civic Education" paper prepared for the Civic Education and Political Participation Workshop, Universite de Montreal, Montreal, June 17-19, 2008

Politikon- (2002)`Post-election Zimbabwe: What next?', *Africa Report No. 93*, 7 June. Available online at: http://www.crisisgroup.org

Ribot, J. C. (2001) Local Actors, Powers and Accountability in African Decentralization: A Review of Issues

Sachikonye, L, 1998, 'Civil Society Organisations in Southern Africa', in Mondaza, I (ed) *Governance and Human Development in Southern Africa*, Harare: Sappho

Spectrum (2009) Zimbabwe: Civil Society and Democracy (NANGO)

Swilling, M. Political Transition, Development and the Role of Civil Society. Paper presented to the Affinity Group for South Africa, American Council of Foundations, Washington, November 6-7, mimeo.

Swilling, Mark. "Political Transition, Development and the Role of Civil Society." Africa Insight 20 (3): 151-168, 1994. Online on www.chra.org

United Development Report, The Human Development Report 2000, Zimbabwe.